The Teacher

"In And Beyond The Classroom"

Veloisa Diana Simpson

Published and Distributed by:
Professional Publishing House
1425 W. Manchester Ave., Suite B
Los Angeles, California 90047
www.professionalpublishinghouse.com
email: professionalpublishinghouse@yahoo.com
(323) 750-3592

First printing: November 2019
ISBN: 978-1-7328982-1-9
10987654321

CONTENTS

To the hundreds of young people whom I have been privileged to teach, to know, and to love, this book is respectfully dedicated.

ABOUT THE AUTHOR

Veloisa Diana Simpson

Veloisa holds a Bachelor of Arts Degree in Education from West Virginia State University.

Veloisa taught for ten years in Indianapolis, Indiana. She decided to move to California to start a new chapter in her life. Veloisa holds a Master's Degree from California Lutheran University. After fulfilling her educational accomplishments, she became employed as a Special Education Teacher for Compton Unified School District (CUSD). Veloisa retired in 1986 from the CUSD. She was honored with a Certificate of Meritorious Service for twenty-seven years of an outstanding contribution and service to CUSD students, staff, and community.

SPECIAL ACHIEVEMENTS

Veloisa received recognition for outstanding classroom techniques in "Behavior Modification." She received a Certificate of Participation in fields testing the Social Learning Curriculum for the Research and Development Center Mental Retardation at Yeshiva University. She was awarded Outstanding Teacher of the Year (from Parents and Student Relationships). The Marquis Who's Who Publication Board certifies that Veloisa Diana Simpson is one of the subjects listed in Who's Who Biographical Record Child Development Professional, First Edition. This inclusion is limited to those individuals who have demonstrated professional competence in their fields of endeavor and who, thereby, contributed significantly to the betterment of contemporary society.

Veloisa has written and been published in several articles in magazines for Special Education. In 1991, she received a Certificate of Appreciation for Reading in Fundamental (RIF) for Outstanding Dedicated Service to the boys and girls of Raymond Avenue Elementary School in Los Angeles, California.

Veloisa Diana Simpson has also written the following books:

Living the Life You Taught Me

Unforgettable Memories

Somewhere Over the Rainbow

People and Friends Remember Me

My Letters to God

See You Later, Alligator

Veloisa is a member of Alpha Kappa Alpha (AKA) Sorority, Inc. and Life Member of Theta Mu Omega, Chapter of Inglewood, California.

BEAUTY

Never lose an opportunity for seeing anything that is beautiful, for beauty is God's handwriting—a wayside sacrament. Welcome it in every face, in every flower, and thank God, for it is a cup of blessing.

SMILE!

BEAUTY

All things bright and beautiful.
All creatures great and small.
All things wise and wonderful.
The Lord God made them all.

SMILE!

LOVE

The greatest happiness in the world is the conviction that we are loved for ourselves, or rather loved in spite of ourselves.

SMILE!

LOVE

It is a beautiful necessity of one's nature to love something.

SMILE!

FRIENDSHIP

A friend is a priceless gem for the crown of life here and a
cherished star in the memory forever.

My friends are little lamps to me.

For every time I lose a friend,

A little lamp goes out.

SMILE!

FRIENDSHIP

Because of a friend, life is a little stronger and fuller. It is a more gracious thing for the friend's existence, whether he be near or far. If the friend is close at hand, that is best, but if he is far away, he still is there to think of, to wonder about, to hear from, to write to, to share life and experience with, to serve, to honor, to admire, to love.

SMILE!

FRIENDSHIP

Beautiful and rich is an old friendship.

There is no friend like the old friend who has shared your days.

What is it to stay young?

It is the ability to hold fast to old friends and to make new ones.

SMILE!

INSPIRATION

Every great and commanding moment in the annals of the world is triumph of some enthusiasm.

SMILE!

INSPIRATION

It takes a lot of patience and God to build a life,

It takes a lot of courage

To meet the stress and strife,

It takes a lot of loving

To make the wrong come right,

It takes a lot of patience and God to build a life.

SMILE!

INSPIRATION

Do not pray for easy living; pray to be stronger. Do not pray for tasks equal to your powers; pray for powers equal to your tasks. Then the doing of your work shall be no miracle, but you shall be a miracle. Every day you shall wonder at yourself, at the richness of life, which has come to you by the grace of God.

SMILE!

COURAGE

He who loses wealth loses much. He who loses a friend loses more, but he who loses his courage loses all.

SMILE!

COURAGE

I have lived to be ninety-five.

I have watched men climb to success, hundreds of them, yet of all of the elements that are important for success, the most important is faith. No great thing comes to anyone unless he has courage.

SMILE!

COURAGE

Do not wish for self-confidence in yourself from others, but get
it from within. Nobody can give it to you. It is one of the greatest
assets of life. Self-confidence comes to you every time you are
knocked down and get up. Keep your fears to yourself, but share
your courage with others.

SMILE!

TRUTH

Truth has no special time of its own.

Its hour is now.

Always.

SMILE!

TRUTH

Honesty of thought, speech and the written word is a jewel. They who curb prejudice and seek honorably to know and speak the truth are the only builders of a better life.

Every great discovery I ever made, I gambled that the truth was there, and then I acted on it in faith that I could prove its existence.

SMILE!

TRUTH

One must learn, day by day, year by year, to broaden your horizons. The more things you are interested in, the more things you enjoy, the more things you are indignant about, the more you have left when anything happens. You must learn, above all, not to waste your soul and happiness. You must learn, above all, not to waste your soul and energy on little things.

I suppose the greatest things in the world is loving people and wanting to destroy the sin and not the sinner. Don't forget; when life knocks you to your knees, that's the best position from which to pray.

That's Where I Learned.

SMILE!

HAPPINESS

Happiness is not in strength, or in wealth, or in power. It lies in ourself, in true freedom, in the conquest of ignoble fear, in perfect self-government, in power of contentment and peace. It lies in the even flow of life, even in poverty, illness, and the very "Valley of the Shadow of Death."

SMILE!

HAPPINESS

Think of the happiness of others, and in this, you'll find your own.

SMILE!

TEACHER
VELOSIA DIANE SIMPSON

I believe in the present and its opportunities in the future. I
believe in its promise. I believe in the divine joy of living.

SMILE!

www.ingramcontent.com/pod-product-compliance
Lightning Source LLC
Chambersburg PA
CBHW071406160426

42813CB00084B/554